EMMANUEL JOSEPH

The Tapestry of Growth, Intertwining Personal, Financial, and Relational Development

Copyright © 2025 by Emmanuel Joseph

All rights reserved. No part of this publication may be reproduced, stored or transmitted in any form or by any means, electronic, mechanical, photocopying, recording, scanning, or otherwise without written permission from the publisher. It is illegal to copy this book, post it to a website, or distribute it by any other means without permission.

First edition

This book was professionally typeset on Reedsy. Find out more at reedsy.com

Contents

1	Chapter 1: Foundations of Personal Growth	1
2	Chapter 2: Cultivating a Growth Mindset	3
3	Chapter 3: The Role of Education and Continuous Learning	5
4	Chapter 4: Financial Literacy as a Cornerstone of Growth	7
5	Chapter 5: Building Wealth through Smart Investments	9
6	Chapter 6: The Interplay of Personal and Financial Growth	11
7	Chapter 7: Effective Communication in Relationships	13
8	Chapter 8: Building Trust and Mutual Respect	15
9	Chapter 9: Financial Planning as a Couple	17
10	Chapter 10: Navigating Life Transitions	19
11	Chapter 11: Balancing Work and Personal Life	21
12	Chapter 12: The Role of Community and Social Networks	23
13	Chapter 13: Overcoming Adversity	25
14	Chapter 14: Setting and Achieving Long-Term Goals	27
15	Chapter 15: Weaving the Tapestry of Growth	29

1

Chapter 1: Foundations of Personal Growth

Personal growth is the bedrock upon which all other aspects of development rest. It encompasses a journey of self-discovery, self-improvement, and self-fulfillment. The foundation of personal growth begins with self-awareness—a deep understanding of one's strengths, weaknesses, values, and aspirations. When individuals are aware of their true selves, they can set meaningful and achievable goals that align with their core values. This chapter explores the importance of self-awareness in laying a strong foundation for personal growth.

Self-awareness is not a destination but an ongoing process. It requires continuous reflection and introspection. By regularly taking time to understand their thoughts, emotions, and behaviors, individuals can identify areas for improvement and recognize patterns that may hinder their growth. This chapter highlights various techniques for cultivating self-awareness, such as mindfulness, journaling, and seeking feedback from others. It emphasizes the need for honesty and vulnerability in this self-exploration journey.

Setting meaningful goals is the next crucial step in personal growth. Goals provide direction and motivation, guiding individuals toward their desired outcomes. This chapter discusses the SMART (Specific, Measurable, Achievable, Relevant, Time-bound) framework for goal-setting, illustrating how it can help individuals create actionable plans. It also explores the significance of setting both short-term and long-term goals, ensuring a balanced approach to personal development.

Personal growth is a lifelong journey, marked by continuous learning and adaptation. As individuals progress in their growth journey, they encounter challenges and setbacks. This chapter underscores the importance of resilience and a growth mindset in overcoming obstacles. It encourages readers to view failures as opportunities for learning and growth, fostering a mindset that embraces change and continuous improvement.

2

Chapter 2: Cultivating a Growth Mindset

A growth mindset is the belief that abilities and intelligence can be developed through dedication, effort, and learning. Unlike a fixed mindset, which views abilities as static and unchangeable, a growth mindset fosters a love for learning and resilience in the face of challenges. This chapter delves into the profound impact of adopting a growth mindset on personal and professional development.

The journey to cultivating a growth mindset begins with understanding the difference between fixed and growth mindsets. Carol Dweck, a renowned psychologist, introduced these concepts through her research on motivation and success. This chapter explores real-life examples of individuals who transformed their lives by shifting from a fixed mindset to a growth mindset. Their stories serve as powerful illustrations of the potential for growth and achievement when one embraces the idea of continuous improvement.

Embracing challenges is a hallmark of a growth mindset. Rather than avoiding difficulties, individuals with a growth mindset see them as opportunities for learning and growth. This chapter provides practical strategies for facing challenges head-on, such as breaking tasks into manageable steps, seeking support from others, and maintaining a positive attitude. It also emphasizes the importance of perseverance and effort in achieving long-term success.

Feedback plays a crucial role in cultivating a growth mindset. Individuals with a growth mindset view feedback as valuable information for improvement rather than as a critique of their abilities. This chapter discusses the significance of seeking constructive feedback, actively listening, and using feedback to refine skills and knowledge. It encourages readers to embrace a mindset of curiosity and continuous learning, ultimately leading to personal and professional growth.

3

Chapter 3: The Role of Education and Continuous Learning

Education is a lifelong journey that extends beyond the confines of formal schooling. It is a dynamic process that fuels personal and professional development, empowering individuals to adapt to an ever-changing world. This chapter explores the transformative power of education and the importance of continuous learning in achieving growth.

The traditional view of education often revolves around formal degrees and certifications. However, this chapter emphasizes that learning is not confined to classrooms and textbooks. It highlights various avenues for education, including online courses, workshops, mentorship, and self-directed learning. By embracing diverse learning opportunities, individuals can acquire new skills and knowledge that enhance their personal and professional lives.

Lifelong learning is essential for staying relevant in today's fast-paced world. This chapter delves into the benefits of continuous learning, such as increased adaptability, improved problem-solving skills, and enhanced creativity. It discusses how lifelong learning contributes to personal growth by expanding horizons and fostering a sense of curiosity. Additionally, it explores the role of learning in professional development, enabling individuals to remain competitive in the job market.

The digital age has revolutionized access to education, making learning opportunities more accessible than ever before. This chapter examines the impact of technology on education, highlighting the proliferation of online learning platforms, educational apps, and virtual classrooms. It also addresses the challenges and opportunities presented by digital learning, encouraging readers to leverage technology to enhance their learning experiences.

The pursuit of education and continuous learning requires a proactive mindset and a commitment to personal growth. This chapter provides practical tips for cultivating a lifelong learning habit, such as setting learning goals, creating a structured learning plan, and seeking diverse perspectives. It emphasizes the importance of staying curious, open-minded, and adaptable in the face of new knowledge and experiences.

4

Chapter 4: Financial Literacy as a Cornerstone of Growth

Financial literacy is the knowledge and understanding of financial concepts that enable individuals to make informed decisions about managing their money. It is a fundamental skill that supports personal stability and relational harmony. This chapter delves into the basics of financial literacy, covering essential topics such as budgeting, saving, investing, and managing debt.

Budgeting is a foundational aspect of financial literacy. It involves creating a plan for how to allocate income and expenses, ensuring that spending aligns with financial goals. This chapter provides practical steps for creating a budget, tracking expenses, and adjusting spending habits. It emphasizes the importance of living within one's means and setting aside funds for emergencies and future needs.

Saving is another crucial component of financial literacy. This chapter explores the benefits of establishing a savings habit, from building an emergency fund to achieving long-term financial goals. It discusses various savings strategies, such as automatic transfers, high-yield savings accounts, and setting specific savings targets. The chapter highlights the importance of prioritizing savings to achieve financial security and peace of mind.

Investing is a powerful tool for growing wealth over time. This chapter introduces readers to different types of investments, including stocks, bonds, real estate, and mutual funds. It explains the principles of risk and return, diversification, and the importance of a long-term perspective. The chapter provides practical advice for beginners, encouraging them to start small, do their research, and seek professional guidance when needed.

Managing debt is essential for maintaining financial health. This chapter discusses the different types of debt, such as credit card debt, student loans, and mortgages. It offers strategies for managing and reducing debt, including creating a repayment plan, consolidating debt, and avoiding high-interest loans. The chapter emphasizes the importance of responsible borrowing and maintaining a good credit score.

5

Chapter 5: Building Wealth through Smart Investments

Investing wisely is key to building wealth and achieving financial independence. This chapter explores various investment options, their potential returns, and the risks associated with each. It provides a comprehensive guide to making informed investment decisions that align with personal financial goals.

Stocks are one of the most common investment options. This chapter explains how stocks represent ownership in a company and the potential for capital appreciation and dividends. It discusses the importance of researching companies, understanding market trends, and diversifying one's portfolio to manage risk. The chapter provides tips for evaluating stocks and making informed investment choices.

Bonds are another popular investment option. This chapter explores the different types of bonds, such as government, municipal, and corporate bonds. It explains how bonds generate income through interest payments and the factors that affect bond prices. The chapter emphasizes the importance of assessing credit risk and choosing bonds that match one's risk tolerance and investment objectives.

Real estate is a tangible investment that can provide both income and capital appreciation. This chapter discusses the benefits and challenges of investing in real estate, from rental properties to real estate investment trusts (REITs). It provides practical advice for evaluating properties, financing options, and managing real estate investments. The chapter highlights the importance of location, market trends, and property management in achieving success.

Mutual funds and exchange-traded funds (ETFs) offer diversified investment opportunities. This chapter explains how these funds pool money from multiple investors to invest in a diversified portfolio of stocks, bonds, or other assets. It discusses the benefits of professional management, diversification, and liquidity. The chapter provides tips for selecting mutual funds and ETFs based on performance, fees, and investment strategy.

6

Chapter 6: The Interplay of Personal and Financial Growth

Personal growth and financial well-being are deeply interconnected, each influencing and supporting the other. This chapter examines the relationship between personal development and financial success, highlighting how they work together to create a fulfilling and balanced life.

Personal development can lead to better financial decisions. This chapter explores how qualities such as self-discipline, resilience, and a growth mindset contribute to effective money management. It discusses the role of self-awareness in recognizing spending habits, setting financial goals, and making informed choices. The chapter emphasizes the importance of aligning financial decisions with personal values and long-term aspirations.

Financial stability, in turn, enhances personal growth. This chapter delves into the psychological aspects of money management, such as the impact of financial stress on mental health and well-being. It discusses how financial stability provides the freedom to pursue personal interests, invest in education, and build meaningful relationships. The chapter highlights the importance of creating a balanced approach to financial and personal development.

The relationship between personal and financial growth is dynamic and cyclical. This chapter explores how personal achievements, such as career advancement and skill development, lead to increased earning potential and financial growth. Conversely, financial achievements, such as paying off debt and building wealth, boost confidence and self-esteem, fueling further personal growth. The chapter encourages readers to view personal and financial growth as complementary and mutually reinforcing.

Creating a holistic growth plan involves integrating personal and financial goals. This chapter provides practical advice for setting and achieving integrated goals, from creating a vision board to tracking progress. It emphasizes the importance of flexibility and adaptability in navigating life's challenges and opportunities. The chapter encourages readers to celebrate their successes and continue striving for balanced growth.

7

Chapter 7: Effective Communication in Relationships

Healthy relationships are built on effective communication, which fosters understanding, trust, and emotional connection. This chapter explores the principles of effective communication and offers practical strategies for improving communication skills in various types of relationships.

Active listening is a cornerstone of effective communication. This chapter discusses the importance of fully engaging in conversations, listening without judgment, and providing feedback. It provides tips for becoming a better listener, such as maintaining eye contact, asking open-ended questions, and summarizing what the other person has said. The chapter emphasizes the value of empathy and validation in building strong connections.

Empathy is the ability to understand and share the feelings of others. This chapter explores the role of empathy in fostering deeper connections and resolving conflicts. It discusses the importance of recognizing and validating emotions, offering support, and showing compassion. The chapter provides practical exercises for developing empathy, such as perspective-taking and practicing non-judgmental acceptance.

Assertiveness is the ability to express one's thoughts, feelings, and needs in a respectful and confident manner. This chapter delves into the principles of assertive communication, including setting boundaries, expressing oneself clearly, and standing up for one's rights. It offers tips for becoming more assertive, such as using "I" statements, maintaining a calm demeanor, and practicing self-awareness. The chapter emphasizes the importance of balancing assertiveness with empathy and respect for others.

Addressing common communication barriers is essential for improving relationships. This chapter identifies common obstacles, such as misunderstandings, assumptions, and emotional triggers. It provides strategies for overcoming these barriers, such as clarifying intentions, seeking mutual understanding, and managing emotions. The chapter encourages readers to practice self-reflection and continuous improvement in their communication skills.

8

Chapter 8: Building Trust and Mutual Respect

Trust and mutual respect are the bedrock of any strong relationship. They create a safe space for individuals to express themselves honestly and openly. This chapter delves into the importance of trust-building activities, transparency, and respect in nurturing healthy relationships.

Building trust takes time and consistent effort. This chapter explores various trust-building activities, such as keeping promises, being reliable, and demonstrating loyalty. It highlights the significance of small, everyday actions in establishing trust and emphasizes the importance of being patient and understanding during this process. The chapter provides practical tips for rebuilding trust when it has been broken, such as offering sincere apologies and making amends.

Transparency is a key component of trust. This chapter discusses the importance of open and honest communication in building transparency. It encourages readers to share their thoughts, feelings, and concerns with their partners, friends, and family members. The chapter also addresses the role of transparency in financial matters, emphasizing the need for clear and open discussions about money, debts, and financial goals.

Mutual respect is essential for maintaining healthy relationships. This chapter delves into the concept of respect, exploring how it involves valuing each other's opinions, boundaries, and individuality. It provides strategies for fostering mutual respect, such as practicing active listening, avoiding judgment, and showing appreciation for each other's contributions. The chapter emphasizes the importance of treating others with kindness and empathy.

Recognizing and addressing trust issues is crucial for relationship growth. This chapter explores common signs of trust issues, such as jealousy, secrecy, and insecurity. It offers practical advice for addressing these issues, including seeking professional help, engaging in open dialogue, and setting boundaries. The chapter encourages readers to work together with their partners to build a foundation of trust and mutual respect.

9

Chapter 9: Financial Planning as a Couple

Money can be a significant source of conflict in relationships, but with proper planning and communication, it can also be a source of strength and unity. This chapter offers guidance on financial planning as a couple, covering topics such as joint accounts, budgeting together, and setting shared financial goals.

Joint accounts can simplify financial management and foster a sense of partnership. This chapter discusses the benefits and challenges of joint accounts, providing tips for managing shared finances effectively. It emphasizes the importance of transparency, trust, and clear communication in handling joint accounts. The chapter also explores alternative arrangements, such as maintaining separate accounts while contributing to joint expenses.

Budgeting together is essential for achieving financial harmony. This chapter provides a step-by-step guide to creating a joint budget, from tracking expenses to setting financial priorities. It discusses the importance of regular budget reviews and adjustments to ensure that both partners are on the same page. The chapter emphasizes the need for compromise and flexibility in managing shared finances.

Setting shared financial goals is crucial for building a strong financial future. This chapter explores the process of identifying and prioritizing joint financial goals, such as saving for a home, planning for retirement, or paying off debt. It provides practical tips for creating a financial plan that aligns with both partners' values and aspirations. The chapter encourages couples to celebrate their financial milestones and support each other in achieving their goals.

Open communication is key to successful financial planning as a couple. This chapter delves into strategies for having productive financial discussions, addressing conflicts, and making joint decisions. It emphasizes the importance of empathy, active listening, and mutual respect in navigating financial challenges. The chapter encourages couples to seek professional financial advice when needed to ensure they are making informed decisions.

10

Chapter 10: Navigating Life Transitions

L ife is full of transitions, and how we navigate them can significantly impact our personal, financial, and relational growth. This chapter addresses major life changes such as career shifts, marriage, parenthood, and retirement, offering practical advice for managing these transitions and maintaining a balanced approach to growth.

Career shifts can be both exciting and challenging. This chapter explores the process of transitioning to a new career, from identifying opportunities to developing new skills. It provides tips for managing the emotional and financial aspects of career changes, such as coping with uncertainty and planning for potential income fluctuations. The chapter emphasizes the importance of resilience, adaptability, and a growth mindset in navigating career transitions.

Marriage is a significant life transition that involves blending personal, financial, and relational aspects. This chapter discusses the importance of open communication, mutual respect, and shared values in building a strong marital foundation. It provides practical advice for managing the financial aspects of marriage, such as combining finances, setting joint goals, and addressing money-related conflicts. The chapter encourages couples to nurture their relationship through ongoing communication and support.

Parenthood is another major life transition that brings both joy and challenges. This chapter delves into the emotional, financial, and relational aspects of becoming a parent. It offers tips for preparing for parenthood, managing childcare expenses, and maintaining a healthy work-life balance. The chapter emphasizes the importance of self-care, support networks, and open communication in navigating the journey of parenthood.

Retirement marks the beginning of a new chapter in life. This chapter explores the financial and emotional aspects of transitioning to retirement, from planning for financial security to finding purpose and fulfillment. It provides practical advice for creating a retirement plan, managing expenses, and staying active and engaged. The chapter encourages readers to embrace this new phase with a positive outlook and a commitment to lifelong growth.

11

Chapter 11: Balancing Work and Personal Life

Achieving a balance between work and personal life is essential for overall well-being and growth. This chapter explores strategies for time management, setting boundaries, and prioritizing self-care, emphasizing the importance of work-life balance in fostering personal growth and maintaining healthy relationships.

Time management is a key factor in achieving work-life balance. This chapter provides practical tips for managing time effectively, such as creating a schedule, setting priorities, and avoiding procrastination. It discusses the importance of allocating time for both work and personal activities, ensuring that neither aspect is neglected. The chapter emphasizes the need for flexibility and adaptability in managing time.

Setting boundaries is crucial for maintaining a healthy balance between work and personal life. This chapter explores the importance of establishing clear boundaries between work and personal activities, such as setting limits on work hours, creating a designated workspace, and minimizing distractions. It provides strategies for communicating boundaries to colleagues and family members, ensuring that they are respected and upheld.

Self-care is essential for overall well-being and growth. This chapter delves into the importance of prioritizing self-care, from physical health to mental and emotional well-being. It offers practical tips for incorporating self-care into daily routines, such as exercise, healthy eating, mindfulness, and relaxation. The chapter emphasizes the need to recognize and address stress and burnout, encouraging readers to seek support and take breaks when needed.

The benefits of work-life balance extend to personal growth and relationships. This chapter explores how achieving a healthy balance between work and personal life fosters personal development, enhances productivity, and strengthens relationships. It discusses the importance of pursuing hobbies, spending quality time with loved ones, and engaging in activities that bring joy and fulfillment. The chapter encourages readers to strive for a balanced and holistic approach to growth.

12

Chapter 12: The Role of Community and Social Networks

Our growth is deeply influenced by the communities and social networks we are part of. This chapter examines the role of social support, community involvement, and networking in personal and professional development. We discuss how to build and nurture supportive relationships that contribute to overall growth.

Social support is essential for emotional well-being and resilience. This chapter explores the importance of having a strong support system, including friends, family, and mentors. It provides tips for cultivating and maintaining supportive relationships, such as being present, offering help, and showing appreciation. The chapter emphasizes the importance of reciprocity and mutual support in building a strong network.

Community involvement provides opportunities for personal and collective growth. This chapter delves into the benefits of participating in community activities, such as volunteering, joining local groups, and attending community events. It discusses how community involvement fosters a sense of belonging, enhances social skills, and contributes to overall well-being. The chapter encourages readers to seek out and engage with their communities.

Networking is a powerful tool for professional growth. This chapter explores the importance of building and maintaining professional networks, both online and offline. It provides practical tips for effective networking, such as attending industry events, joining professional organizations, and leveraging social media. The chapter emphasizes the value of genuine connections and the importance of giving as much as receiving in networking relationships.

The role of community and social networks extends to personal development as well. This chapter discusses how positive relationships and social interactions contribute to personal growth by providing support, inspiration, and opportunities for learning. It highlights the importance of surrounding oneself with positive influences and being an active participant in one's social network. The chapter encourages readers to nurture their relationships and seek out new connections that align with their growth goals.

13

Chapter 13: Overcoming Adversity

A dversity is an inevitable part of life, but it can also be a catalyst for growth. This chapter shares stories of resilience and provides strategies for coping with challenges. We highlight the importance of a positive outlook, adaptability, and the support of loved ones in overcoming difficult times.

Resilience is the ability to bounce back from setbacks and challenges. This chapter explores the qualities that contribute to resilience, such as optimism, flexibility, and perseverance. It provides practical tips for developing resilience, such as setting realistic goals, maintaining a positive attitude, and seeking support. The chapter emphasizes the importance of self-compassion and self-care in building resilience.

A positive outlook is crucial for overcoming adversity. This chapter discusses the power of positive thinking and the impact of mindset on how individuals perceive and respond to challenges. It provides strategies for cultivating a positive outlook, such as practicing gratitude, focusing on solutions, and reframing negative thoughts. The chapter encourages readers to adopt a growth mindset and view challenges as opportunities for learning and development.

Adaptability is essential for navigating change and uncertainty. This chapter delves into the importance of being open to change and willing to adapt to new circumstances. It provides tips for becoming more adaptable, such as embracing flexibility, staying curious, and being proactive in seeking solutions. The chapter highlights the role of creativity and innovation in finding new ways to overcome obstacles.

Support from loved ones is invaluable during times of adversity. This chapter explores the importance of seeking and accepting support from friends, family, and mentors. It discusses the role of social support in providing emotional comfort, practical assistance, and motivation. The chapter encourages readers to build and maintain strong support networks and to be there for others in their times of need.

14

Chapter 14: Setting and Achieving Long-Term Goals

Long-term goals provide direction and purpose, guiding individuals toward their desired outcomes. This chapter offers a roadmap for setting and achieving meaningful goals, emphasizing the importance of persistence, flexibility, and celebrating milestones along the way.

The process of setting long-term goals begins with self-reflection. This chapter explores the importance of understanding one's values, passions, and aspirations in creating meaningful goals. It provides practical tips for identifying long-term goals, such as creating a vision board, writing down goals, and breaking them into smaller, actionable steps. The chapter emphasizes the need for clarity and specificity in goal-setting.

Persistence is key to achieving long-term goals. This chapter discusses the importance of staying committed and motivated, even in the face of challenges and setbacks. It provides strategies for maintaining persistence, such as setting realistic timelines, tracking progress, and staying focused on the bigger picture. The chapter encourages readers to develop a growth mindset and to view obstacles as opportunities for learning and growth.

Flexibility is essential for adapting to changing circumstances and adjusting goals as needed. This chapter explores the importance of being open to change and willing to reassess and adjust goals when necessary. It provides tips for staying flexible, such as regularly reviewing goals, seeking feedback, and being willing to pivot when needed. The chapter highlights the importance of balancing persistence with adaptability.

Celebrating milestones is crucial for staying motivated and recognizing progress. This chapter discusses the significance of acknowledging and celebrating achievements along the way. It provides practical tips for celebrating milestones, such as rewarding oneself, sharing successes with others, and reflecting on the journey. The chapter encourages readers to appreciate their progress and to continue striving for their long-term goals.

15

Chapter 15: Weaving the Tapestry of Growth

In the concluding chapter, we bring together the threads of personal, financial, and relational development. We reflect on the interconnected nature of these aspects and provide a holistic view of growth. The chapter encourages readers to embrace the journey, celebrate their progress, and continue striving for a balanced and fulfilling life.

Personal growth is the foundation of overall development. This chapter revisits the importance of self-awareness, continuous learning, and a growth mindset in achieving personal fulfillment. It emphasizes the need for ongoing self-reflection and adaptation in the pursuit of personal growth. The chapter encourages readers to set meaningful goals and to view personal development as a lifelong journey.

Financial growth is a crucial component of overall well-being. This chapter highlights the significance of financial literacy, smart investments, and responsible money management in achieving financial stability and independence. It underscores the importance of aligning financial decisions with personal values and long-term goals. The chapter encourages readers to take control of their financial future and to view financial growth as an integral part of their overall development.

Relational growth is essential for building strong, supportive, and fulfilling relationships. This chapter explores the importance of effective communication, trust, and mutual respect in nurturing healthy relationships. It emphasizes the role of social support, community involvement, and networking in personal and professional growth. The chapter encourages readers to invest in their relationships and to view relational growth as a vital aspect of their overall well-being.

The interconnected nature of personal, financial, and relational growth is the essence of a balanced and fulfilling life. This chapter brings together the insights and strategies from previous chapters, offering a holistic view of growth. It encourages readers to embrace the journey, celebrate their progress, and continue striving for a balanced and fulfilling life. The chapter concludes with a call to action, inspiring readers to take charge of their growth and to weave their own tapestry of development.

Book Description:

"The Tapestry of Growth: Intertwining Personal, Financial, and Relational Development" is a comprehensive guide that explores the interconnected nature of personal, financial, and relational growth. Through 15 insightful chapters, this book provides practical strategies, real-life examples, and actionable advice for achieving balanced and fulfilling development in all aspects of life.

Readers will embark on a journey of self-discovery and personal growth, learning the importance of self-awareness, continuous learning, and a growth mindset. They will gain valuable insights into financial literacy, smart investments, and responsible money management, empowering them to achieve financial stability and independence. The book also delves into the principles of effective communication, trust-building, and mutual respect, offering practical tips for nurturing healthy and supportive relationships.

From setting and achieving long-term goals to navigating life transitions and overcoming adversity, "The Tapestry of Growth" provides a holistic approach to growth that embraces the complexities of modern life. Whether you're seeking personal fulfillment, financial success, or stronger relationships, this book offers the tools and inspiration to weave your own tapestry of development and create a balanced and enriching life.

www.ingramcontent.com/pod-product-compliance
Lightning Source LLC
LaVergne TN
LVHW020739090526
838202LV00057BA/6133